After It All, I'll Just Say This, …

Poetry for Moments.

By
Jordan Thiel

Jordan Thiel was born in 1971 and then immediately sent to live in Kuna, Idaho, as was the style at the time. It was a tiny town of just under 1,000 people, with only one grocery store and no stoplights. Now, it's 20 times that size, has many thriving stoplights, and has two – count 'em – TWO grocery stores. There, Jordan gained the knowledge he needed from the repeated, consecutive parades Kuna would hold: one decrying abortion, and the next decrying feeding the unaborted. (Just kidding. It's a nice town. But, yeah, they did hold those parades.) He went on to study nothing even remotely helpful to his writings. He enjoys the shackles of married life, and the pleasures of eating the seafood his wife refuses to touch. He is childless and barren, but does – … keep this info away from other men – put on party hats to celebrate the birthdays of his pets.

Table of Contents

Good Struggle

We speak of heroes
Who moved mounts,
Carried the victim,
Gave food,
And brought daylight,
But, must preface all with,
"He's dead now", and,
"But she's been gone for so long".
Their recognition is braced and bracketed
By and to the time when we lack
What they provided,
Only when our feet slip,
Our mouths are dry,
Our mind dulls.
And, that instant, brings
Happenstance to your soul.
See the challenge?
See that need?
Heroes did not miss hard work for goals.
So may you do.
Glance to look,
And say "no".
No matter the sphere,
And the numbers in it,
—Even you, alone—
Grapple with that thorn bush,
Twist and maneuver
Until the cuts and blood bring
Your demon to demise,

And you can only then take breaths,
Breaths for relaxation,
Breaths free.
Even heroes collapse
At the end,
And cry from the battle.
But do, with time,
Rise,
Stand,
Share.
Others need to see this moment,
They, the saved,
Or, they, the next hero.
There is hope in that vision.
There is belief in self in that moment.
Rest, Savior, and relish,
But,
Give that rest reason
In rising.

No Trade Worth This

Hope and self-love come from the same source,
One cannot be taken from the heart
Without expense to the other.
While not twins,
With their interior intricacies of identity,
They breathe the same air, and
Depend upon the same nutrients.
Were I to stand on the edge,
Having passed across all,
I would, oh, so,
Have needed both.
To accept one's heart and self, Child,
Means to look at the end,
See what can be,
And what you wish
As free for your taking.
As day and eve weigh down,
Set you on your back in the mud,
Knowing that your new morning comes,
And that things can be fixed,
Serves as a kindness to every soul.
It's a battle plan,
I know,
But what a battle you are worth.
No linkage or lock can't be broken
With a sight to set upon,
And the stores of strength you've built.
The way is probably trod,
Foot and claw marks along,

By those who crossed this way,
With a burden like yours,
And their own tears to dry.
Like the Titans and Gods,
You bring marks to this struggle
Where seeing leads to being,
Where your hand may touch
The hand print of a divinity.
How broken is one,
Forced into a hopeless moment,
Seeing their worth as a pittance.
Be not so,
Be not so,
Be not so.
You may never stand higher,
Or run faster,
Lift more,
But
You can give all your tiny frame has
To your hopes and trust.
Smile at the mirror.
No matter the changes,
Smile at yourself.
Damn the politicians
And those preachers of the blasphemous.
Turn your cheek from them,
Taking no strike,
Even at their guidelines,
For you have yourself as your earnest friend,
Lest all abandon you to those voices.
You are who you are, so let be what you may be.

It's not into roles we must pretend
For hope and self-love to rise,
But 'tis authenticity we embrace
For either to be as currency in our lives.
We wish you that sweet direction,
though we do not walk with you,
For you set it, with your heart,
And in that,
Let each night's rest build you up.
Let each night's rest bring dreams to life.

Plenty

Do fat women know that they
Are unattractive?
Do they understand
That from screen,
To magazine,
To poster,
They are not what men see?
They fall short
And sob
In never reaching
That pedestal,
And they can shrink into hardness.
And, in this,
It is
Men
That fall short.
As if women are meant for this,
To be a definition of beauty
And nothing more.
In this,
It is men
That fall short.
The lines stretch to the horizon,
As women pine, wait, and bleed to
Be the thing, the evident thing
Men want,
As if women are meant for this.
Love inevitably becomes
A complication,

Where legs and breasts
Are not enough,
Where long, flowing hair
Holds no answers.
A woman, fat,
Though driven to insecurity,
Can say the words of support,
Those, as men, we seek
And should seek.
There is work to be done,
Scores of burdens
That cannot be swept away,
But women,
As a woman, you
Need not have a glorious
Look
To see and hold our burden
On your shoulders
With us.
Evil label,
You of plus size,
By that, you are an outlier
From norm and purpose.
By that, you need more to be wanted.
Evil label,
Plus size,
By that,
You lack permission
To shop
With the thin and fit.
Evil label, evil.

Do fat women know
They have no value as models?
But, do they know
They need none?
Men, take a soft hand, caring eyes,
Take conversation and surprise,
Take adoration,
And judge your porn stars
With such.
Need for a night
Pales with the ongoing days,
And evaporates when
Our insecurities
Need mending.
Fat women,
Be the meaningfulness
To souls,
And let slip
That thin promise of
Some erotic demand.
For, in truth,
I tell you, woman,
Even to call you fat is evil,
As if you are,
Once more,
Not as you should be.
So, you are a woman,
And playing the part
Of that empty, manly demand
Will never lead
Anywhere,

Like being the one you are
And its satisfaction.
In thoughts and words, be.
In your dreams, be.
Let the vapid impulses
Of men fall short,
This time,
And each day beyond.
Let men fall with their dolls
Of fitness,
Where they gain
No guarantee of
Connection with a mate.
I cannot promise
That men will see their error.
I give promise that it is man's error.

To the Sides of the Statue of You

I'm content to wallow here,
Where your shadow once fell,
While others huddle 'round your grave,
As if it meant anything to you.
I'm under our tree,
Feeling the worn knot
That supported your back
While you leaned against my side.
I know your locations of dreams,
Lands you sought to see,
And those you once saw,
And were thrilled.
But while you were here,
Your life was in these hallways, upon that chair,
Under that blanket, shadowed on that porch.
The ideal,
Where you wear the flowing dress,
White adornments, in hair and upon toe,
Walking in bright light,
On tiptoes,
Like an Angel,
Yes, that ideal, portrayed by them.
But I'll lie next to your pillow
Where you were sick,
Where you refused
To let anyone see your hair in disarray,
Where I spooned soup in for your meal,
So you could keep your hands wrapped,
Warm,

Under cover.
I'll stand on the driveway
Where you cursed the flat tire,
Asked me to fix it,
Before your friends missed you at the bar.
While others chat about some eternal path
You are supposed to now be on,
I'll, rather, step softly on
The surrounding sidewalks
That carried our conversation along.
Let me miss these that are tiny.
Let me ponder upon your blinks,
As well as upon your gaze.
Let me pause upon
That small breath you take in,
The moment before whispering,
"I love you".
Let the parades for you,
And the implications of forever,
Wile away the time of others.
While I, only, know who you were,
And where.

____

Make Up Your Mind

Into each life
Is the new from recycling,
Is the trying of those elements
To forgo and forget
Their old cycles and patterns.
Each caught breath
Stands either in unison
With those dead,
Or varies to
Thrill existence.
Stand on the line,
Walk it, dirge,
In a row of like beings, and
Carry on tradition
Despite urges.
This path to purpose,
Built by the tiny grains
Of consensus,
Can carry you on,
To repeated, glorious times.
However, something is lost
In that packed procession.
Electrons, bored
With that same tug,
With the same orbit,
With the same decay rate,
Seek to assert
And tread
On undisturbed dirt,

Where no queue is
Directed, where
There is no recognition.
Over the next rise,
You can go.
Yearn to be, Star-child,
Not
What has been
In succession.
Speak, and
Speak again where
Others have told
You to be quiet.
Laugh to laugh,
Not to laugh
As you should,
With the viewers.
Carbon, carbon, we all
Shall always be the same
In the DNA,
But, and thus,
To live our choices
— Ours, —
To be the random
Outlier that never was
Before,
Brings that new
Pleasure to
Timeless particles and
Light speed beams,
For they are

Then where they longed
To go.

____

Defeat, Be Gone

It's not all bad to face the misery,
Abandon the hope because of heaviness,
When we can't see a trail ahead of us,
Through the crippling presence of circumstances of
our woe.
The fade of fortune leaves us alone with ourselves.
The panic, that anger, all this in our thoughts,
Thoughts that are only for us.
If we are to step forward, climb, reach,
Gain footing and achieve through that trouble,
It is truly our own self that makes it so.
There is no authentic example to follow when we
are without,
Seeing no ground as possible to traverse.
That is not all that bad to discover.
It is my foot I must raise and plant down
In my desired direction,
Without knowing if I'll succeed.
I can move, but alone, only myself, with the drive.
We come to hear "this is me", all coming from
within.
Rebuild,
Reclaim,
Or, create anew,
All from yourself.
Tragedy is not opportunity to be sought.
But it comes.
It is the unfortunate destruction of who we have
been

And all we wanted.
But to have that spark in our mind,
To learn of yourself,
Inspired only by yourself,
Discovering the essential,
Honest
Intent of who we are,
Not known before,
It is a joy.
"I have lost", we whisper,
And then, we can find more that is not lost.
Able to peer through the smoky fog
At some dwindling light,
Finding it familiar, then saying "I will go there".
The strength of walking through the ache and
wounds,
Ignoring that urge to wallow,
You can hear the beating of your heart with such
effort,
Your lungs that choked on destruction moments
ago,
Fill now with air to calm you,
And set it right.
Being defeated is being alone.
Then, alone, we can grasp that strength.
Not as victor above other men,
But,
We can be the victor above what we were,
When the top came down, the flame rose,
And we were consumed.
No, there is nothing pleasant in

That place where our hope flies away.
But hope does not drive us onward.
It is our worth that does this.
While we cannot know if things will be alright,
We can know that our self,
Alone,
Can make it right.
Brush the remaining soot.
Build, knowing you can.

___

A View

There, this distance from being warned of the pain, to the knowing and experiencing of that pain, is where you may exist at your peril. Inside there, hope remains, solace is sought expectantly, and perceived outcomes are bright. There, we do not lack consideration of the pain, but we push back against it, saying, "We can do more! We can do more." Remedy of our thorns is never seen as temporary... it is embraced as the solution. But, like the futility of pushing on the front of a speeding train to stop it, the pain arrives, with averted warning, and with a severing of hope, solace, and brightness.

But,

That instant of being torn asunder brings a choice:

We can choose to be filled with the pain, as the disappointments of this valley mount, where the more we gave comes up for naught and we look at our empty palms and fingers, worked to callous for nothing;

Or,

Just maybe, a spark of memory will build from tiny ember to a roaring blaze, where we see all that has occurred. There we can replay what was before, what there was in the ensuing onslaught of days in joy and love that never for a moment stopped by in our heart — that remains now, giving reason to the pain. And, in that, understand that reason.

Would we give anything to abandon that agony now tight around our soul? No. Such is to deny the love that bound, and binds, us to the lost. So, weep. Do not seek laughter in reminiscence, do not long that this goes away, and do not reach for a swift end. Weep until your cheeks are wet and the handkerchief full. You deny nothing. You hold onto everything. Is pain sure? Yes, with your satisfaction. In this acceptance, we are still with that — with those — who have slipped away. Our calloused hands will never give up the sense of their departed touch. We can wave goodbye, rather than cling to emptiness. We can take our step forward rather than become stuck fast with painful weight. There is reason for our connections in life. Never forget.

Blink, Prefaced

Life
Racing by, sauntering, walking, crawling,
Is out of our control.
Though, there is strength,
Repute,
In the wavering and struggle, onward.
For life, uncontrolled, need not,
Should not,
Define us.
Where we could stare up to the clouds,
Howl at their existence,
That choice is not ours
To remove them.
Yet, bring your eyes to a place
It is possible to go,
Not up into that sky
Where only our whines and blubbering can
venture.
That choice to go either this way or
That,
Resides.
Whether it be,
In mid ocean,
Upon isolated sand dune,
Through storms and winds,
On iceberg,
Or, in shadow of mountains,
We still can look forward,
Find and name our own goal.

Extend our own hand that will
Steady the tumult along the trek.
While we find it confused,
And ourselves surprised,
Scream to thine own self
"I am! Life is!
Accept this, embrace this, take it in.
There are still paths to use!
Still ways forward!"
How, when down,
Ease tends us still.
It holds stuck like a chain.
By your heart,
Don't cease because it is
There.
When stuck and held,
You must strain and suffer,
Pull to bring yourself to your feet,
Toward that place you see.
Better, yes, to be the constant motion,
Avoid that snare.
But, when that is where you are,
Don't drop your gaze.
Step on until ease breaks, and chains dissolve,
And then growth can continue.
Find that definition of who you shall be
On the way,
And find a little comfort.
That wandering goal is there, far or near,
And you shall,
Can,

Have it.
No need to follow the line of crowds.
No hurry to be first to their own aims.
No sense to not being who you are
When you are looking forward.
Be in control,
Suffer,
Strain,
When the wild and unsavory comes.
Though it comes, uncontrolled,
It is still your
Life.

Unborn

You, that never will be,
I lament this fact.
To not lie, in my youth, and of legal years, I
Did not see you in slumber, and in visions
In the daily life I rushed through.
So, it is now, that, though I name you,
Though I glance your image,
Suppose your voice,
Now, then, I find a hole you never left there
Is there.
Should time be bent so I could return?
Should that I go back there to my start,
Would that all my indiscretions
Would fly away, apart,
I would bring you 'round, that time,
Into this being I just
Now see needs to be?
The tiny fingers of the hand
You extend to me, and the new, so
New, cry for warmth and care,
It would be beauty and horror to
See you mine.
To hear you try to make the new word,
Such helpless pleasure in my
Inability to do it for you,
Could be that etching in this journal
I would keep of you.
Up stretched arms of beckoning are sure
To take my breath away,

For you want me,
As I am, wanted by you,
To help you fly,
As your giggle makes this heart fly,
Not alone again,
Never to be,
For I would be wanted by you.
There are books I counted well
In my own childhood self,
Ones taken in through silence
Or the recital of those my parents,
Holding flint-to-steel
Of those thoughts
You would not have without them,
Deeds you need to know can be,
Books I'd share, over and over,
Till we together could speak them
In unison.
Would that such a library was to be yours.
I'd know pain, that I'd know,
As you feel them, causing mine,
Where the moments freeze
And I wonder and wish if
The next minute will come
With relief or tragedy.
Stuck would that time be as you cried
Again,
And I would apply feeble words to you
In your wound,
Hoping that nearly mentioning them
Would make you whole, eternal,

Never needing them again, so
You could stand forever smiling
At me.
We, walking, gripping each,
Can hear that sound of the season,
One to give beyond the tinsel,
Paper, Gold, ribbon,
Where our dime can be more than squirreled
In piggy bank or pocket,
And we hear that sound.
You ask, pleasing questioning,
To be given to give,
And I relent, without any hesitant
Thought.
But, at this dream,
You burst and are ashes,
And I am now, now,
In this terrible hour where you are not.
You will never hear the bell ringer
Or that dime settle into his kettle,
And I will never hear the beg
And those steps you take towards it,
Never to hold my hand,
Never to need my comforting rambling,
Never feel your weight on these shoulders.
You, my child, should have
Been my choice and desire.
Instead, I didn't, in fact
And in face of that you should have become,
And meant to me.
There are trundle beds and toys and

Smart outfits and lunchboxes and candy
And hiking shoes and pizzas and
Rocking horses and nightlights and a world
Full of promise I need to you to need
Right now,
And they are ghosts that vex me,
In this terrible, empty room
Full of mine,
None of yours,
For I cannot bring you now from
My hopes,
Where you sit, smiling, while I look upon you,
Not to be.
You, my eyes, my ears, my voice,
Bound for a formless memory that will
End at my death,
Where the essence of your absence
Is loss,
In my life,
Where you are so lost
To my loss.

Busy or Bust

Between your blinks,
Life happens.
As you pull a breath from rest,
Shock on an away continent
Speeds present beginnings and end.
Your empty mind and hand
Do not mean a lack of existence.
As the frantic businessman,
Arriving home,
Longing for the recliner,
Removing tie and dress shoe,
Feels that tug on his leg
Every minute or two,
And he states,
"One minute please."
"One more minute,"
And he misses her say
"Dad, Barbie got new shoes today",
Her hand extended up, waving the things a bit.
We say, cliche and romantic,
"My heart will go on".
But,
Where will we send it,
And what do we give it to carry?
Do words or lack simply flow through the mind
And soul,
Or is that scant weight one of consequence?
Do our sentences
Said in disdain,

Convince the youthful gang member,
That he is now
What he always will be?
Do we flee disaster,
Showing the woman — feeble — upon the floor
The importance we give to
The troubles of others?
Where will caring and pleasure go,
When Dad insists that Barbie
Will have to wait?
Things go somewhere,
On and on.
Words and acts believed,
They change hopes and hearts.
They go wild and out of control.
Between our blinks,
They strike a match we did not know
Was within our hand.
From within the misunderstanding
And misinterpretation,
Are shivers upon the plans and aspirations.
We cannot be one with,
The weight of abandoned minutiae,
As we are told,
With frustration and head upon pillow,
Not now,
Despite who you are.

Untitled (In Place)

Here,
Not there,
You cannot grow,
And you cannot be more,
But you need not be less.
Held fast by the wall
We cannot even peer over,
There is nowhere to go on,
On to where your next dream rests.
Do not retreat to your path,
Back, knowing you will face
The wrath of legion
To regain this place you hold.
In this forced term of waiting,
Comes a gift,
A moment where plans should be laid
And made strong by reality.
Without seeing the way forward,
Plan for what may be on that way,
And by that daydream,
Let desire enlarge and improve
While you are made still here.
So, stand firm in this spot,
And watch.
Stand firm and watch.
Look for the seam in the wall
That buckles, as all walls do,
And slip on, then.
Fate, all that converges,

Is seen in the consequences
And not in the schemes.
Let all you can do
Be all you do,
And don't look to fate for permission.
Don't fret this barrier.
There will be more walls ahead
And corresponding moments of pause.
It is the path that forms fate,
It is the wait that gives purpose
To what has become real.

To Die

And when my end has snared me
In the tightness of its fist,
Not to release me again,
Let me lie upon a pillow, looking at you,
Hearing music next to my ear,
Of Lissie, so I can know that
Angels will call on me.
Yes, let me know that lie,
Lest I scream at the developing darkness,
Or whisper "No" in a way you find frightening.
Give me Molly's Cub to comfort me with its pelt.
Show me pictures of Miller's run,
Jack's patience, Jill's spin,
Jemaine's jump, Eddie's nuzzle, Missie's satiety,
Sasha's smile, JoJo's zoomies,
Haley's begs, Demi's happy eyes,
And, always, Zorba's forgiveness.
Let me see you wear my ring.
Let me feel your kiss as I fade.
Make that time something I'd remember,
Could I remain and bask in past days.
I can't promise I'll go anywhere
In the finality of eternal hope,
But I promise,
Your dearness and support will be the whole of my
focus,
As I go.

―――――――――――――――――――――――――

Pack

These viscous animals, docile,
We have taken an army of them into
Our arms.
With that wordplay,
They were ours to command
And to use,
But we did not.
Despite that Bible,
In spite of them being counted food and
Tools,
And, true, relinquishing all abuse,
We loved them, and love all.
No,
Instinct may be,
And animal each one,
But emotion, hope, thrill, caring, sadness,
In their display,
Through day and eve,
We discovered,
Lighting our eyes beyond
Ownership unto kinship,
Through their name being unique
To their heart and mind within.
Long do those happy selves run in
Our thoughts,
And long they shall forever chase us
Till our end,
Each being a different friend, allowed
To be individuals

In this pack.
Yes, long will be their path along ours,
Careening down trails, into lakes,
Holding pace to the threshold
They know,
Being aside me and her,
In rest and dreaming.
I laugh in missing presence to that
Trusting cuddle and the head resting upon my
Thigh, and such pain in this
And more
Is lovely, and more.
And more,
They are friends
That I miss.
They could not share our secrets, revealing
In veritas those acts of humanity,
But would not, could it be their tongue
Was ours, holding tight that bond
That we had.
We would walk through thorns,
Burn down the immense forest
That separates their place they stand
From ours,
Would tear down walls and swim a fearful
Ocean,
All that their fur would touch our hands.
In nightmare,
We have done as much
With only morning, awakening,
Holding answer that we cannot

Do so.
Fury is called for and, yet, set aside,
In lieu, and because of their life,
A peaceful reminiscence of all we once
Had, and carry into each promised hour.
Were,
Had they been beasts,
Were
Their lives savage,
They would still be tame in our soul,
In that,
They were not so to us, and
They were not so.
When given choice and chance,
They were not so.

Blow On

Sincerity is blustered by the winds of time, and, so, our resolve may fade.
It can hold on fast to little, as such, but those that are little are important,
Important enough to stick, while the less-than trivial splinter away,
Leaving us all the more sincere in our exposed and vulnerable moments.
Some scheduled fancy flies away as we suddenly need our home, our loves,
If they will have us for having entered the winds we battle now.
"Let me see my wife again", we wail,
"Let me hold my pet, feel the hand of my mother,
See the sun set fall upon my favorite mount, look upon La Pieta' in soft light,
And know what makes me grin!"
This is the wind at work, its design, to tear us to our core where we are ourselves
And we are left with what makes us real.
Fly away games and gluttony, then be followed by grandeur and status
In this terrible trial we unknowingly needed.
Only in the impending end do we think and dwell upon what cannot be set aside
Without leaving our own whole being to be lost in the tempest.
Then, if the winds relent and we are left in a sunny calm,

May that be our moment to show remaining
resolve, to bind our life to what we need most,
And make bright, new goals to follow on the
sustaining elements of our lives.
So, lest the storm returns and buffets us, we then
have true means and reason to survive.

This Throng

You were right, Upton, you diviner of greed,
We are in The Jungle,
Couched in our beaten down
State,
Again and again,
Of self-confidences
And self-reliances.
Chasing the crumb in
Lifetime pursuit.
Holding the knife in defense and
Never in feast.
Where we go is no safety by meter,
Treading among our predator
And prey, holding tight
Our teeth, we are at war,
Started by wealth above us,
Where we have no part or party.
Where that war
Forces us to soldier this remaining strength
For no gains,
And his and hers
Are only whispers of the dying.
Dirty, the man sleeps, then wakes
In no chance to clean, and
Dirty he sleeps, then wakes,
Then dreams of pure sleep were
Set aside is his horror for no morsel
Of somber repose.
Slowly shall lad and lass

Regard themselves or
Fellows they brush shoulders with on
The worn path,
Worn
By the fuel for the fire,
Generations of that fuel, dirty and short
Lived.
Ours is no place for civility
As it takes a moment already bought
In horrible trade in trade, while
Giving all for absence and empty purse,
It has no place.
Backs are broken in a day of such
Hazy world and hovel,
And no mansion promised,
Hence, not dreamt,
Will open to
Us.
We have nothing to grasp,
Taken in the war, declared and sure,
Yet,
Denied by rulers.
Denied in intent to make us long
For the more that exists in a bank
Where we are but deposits,
And there shall what is ours rot,
Said to be of nothing
In our arms,
And shines only in others.
This lot, this throng
Of agony, invented intentionally for

Our bonds to be unseen.
Hope on, Miss and Mister,
And your children suffer with their
Youth,
Promised to land owners and producers at birth,
Of another world, never theirs.
The dead-in-waiting whisper.
Where they have been,
Claiming soulful events of dolls
And those there of deterioration.
They, who will die, embrace belief
That
This Jungle would let them be who
They would,
And they would not be without
This Jungle,
In foolish and allowed imaginings,
Forgetting the war they fought and lost
All they were to a penny,
For a penny.

____

Hello, At the Bar

Striving with presence,
Trying among voices,
Needing from the mass,
To be one of the assembly,
One that belongs.
Rather the rest in the corner with solitude.
"I come from nothing",
He would tell them.
They can tell,
Without his words.
"I come from nothing,
But is nothing what I deserve?"
"Can I stand near as I finish my drink?
Feign conversation as you laugh
And as I long to know you."
He stands near, hoping
"I'll be next to you, and I'll be with you."
So,
With recognition,
I speak to him.
"Doing well?"
"Need anything?"
His eyes, somewhere in shock,
As he wonders
If he was noticed,
Or if he was in my way in
His oft visits here,
Being part of the flow, through the door,
To the bar,

To the stool.
So, I know his face.
But his shock stands shy,
Still.
He gives some quick quip,
Says "Leaving too early,
Leaving immediately."
Still,
We shake hands.
I say "Nice to see you."
But
He replies genuinely,
From his sleeve,
"Thank you. Thanks so much."
No change to his world.
No tectonic change to who he is,
Or, who I have become to him.
He might see me as little,
But
He will remember that a voice
In his presence,
Was better than the silence upon his stool.

Look Elsewhere, Lad

This is not inspirational.
Your ways will not change with my words.
The furthest my sentences will reach is the distance
and the time it takes for you to notice when I
appeared.
Within myself are the moldings and gears you do
not have, the muscles built of experiences you find
incompatible and strange.
I have not lived for you to follow, for as I stepped
forward, the leaves and branches and grasses
snapped back into place with no trace that I
advanced or the notion you need to seek me here.
If I were to be who I want to be, which I seek, I
can't be anything like anyone else, so I won't leave
any phrases to give you hope, rendering you alone
in your own strength.
As we cried out upon entry into this world, my
voice had a pitch which never was resounded by
you, or by another, and was not meant to be.
Though I point, I gesture, I clasp, I pull, I snap, I
beckon,
Though the where-with-all of my needy logics in
those moments is based somewhere, subtly,
among the pieces of a puzzle come from millions of
people,
Your own hand is at its own interest, sharing no
part of how I acted.
I miss and lack so much, and all that is wide open to
you, no need for copying me.

In your reach are yours, as mine are at arm's
length, held above and beyond,
Simply because I was not on a stage.
I was not on display for mimicry,
And my unworthy, dissatisfying ways hopefully
miss your attention,
And my mistakes you might step around on your
own.
Do not think I will hold you up, upright, for I
scarcely can do this for myself.
I am not some sort of model, but, if I am one, you
don't have the glue that keeps me together, so
look to your own pieces.
I do not share your shadow.
Though we face the same sun and shade our eyes
with caps, I spy that which you didn't notice.
Though we face the same trials, the lessons of my
parents, absent from yours, lead on to places you
can't imagine.
It is enough in me that I breathe, and that this air I
take in is mine, and that you must take in the
other.
Leave me in your wake, as I seek to make and
escape my own.
This is not inspirational.

Her Eyes Closed

My emotions are flammable
and I feel the numbness of shock.
They break down so quickly,
Just as our eyes get used to their light.
Then the real closes in.
We stare, see lifelessness.
We teeter between before and after,
Finding after empty,
Finding nothing to hold, to love,
To satisfy.
That need burns,
Lighting the bonfire,
Bonfire, heavy loss,
Lighting the recollections we don't want to lose.
But we are after,
After that accrual of daily bits of joy,
The loss threatens a loss,
Threatens our mind
To worry if what we see is all that will be after.
Will our being with, now without,
be that which takes away our memories?
Day after night,
Will the daily, minuscule cloud our sight
To before?
Seeing only what was.
Not having.
My emotions are flammable
And I fear the numbness of realizing
This moment.

Name

Why does this need a name?
As if it is just one thing to me.
My hopes, my swaying emotions,
My desires to be, my rustled repentances,
My ruminations.
I must name them?
I have to give it a coat of paint you enjoy?
Some tint you can understand?
Without that name, is it not valid?
Did I live in vain until I named it?
Damn.
You change it with a title that fits you,
because it no longer is what
I hoped,
I felt,
I desired,
I regretted,
I dwelt upon.
I know, now, nothing I share belongs to my mind.
Nothing belongs to me.
Because you want them to be known by a name
you can accept.
I had to twist them to be called this name.
Why,
they are already named by me as I think them.
What is it to me if you don't know
Their colors in here?
Their names in here?
Call them what you want.

But I will not name them for you.

Maligna

Man,
Taken by vice, punished by cancers.
Not racked, but burnt,
Not racked, but burnt,
On a porch facing east from the sunset
Watching all go to dark,
While still there, but not visible.
The ill grapples with the mind,
Shouting
"Where will I go if not held back?"
The mind leans silent.
No retort or word can pinpoint
Or possess the worry.
Were Man to shake and tremble,
Run to and fro,
And peek from around a corner,
Still,
There is mind and there is ill.
Would that this inactive heart be remedy,
Would that the ocean surface be not rough,
Would that this sand ran slow and thick,
All set to a place where dreams stood fast.
But, not to be.
Would they, but not to be.
To count remaining days within this gentle tempest
Grows not some number,
And, though the Man tries,
Leaves a calendar of erased days
And worn scribbles.

Light the match and inhale,
Needlessly inhale,
For where he is, it is pointless to stop now.
Songs of anger? No.
Songs of joyful glee? No.
Songs … any songs? No.
Just listen to the strife,
Where ill and mind roll upon the problem,
Bringing up dust not yet turned to mud by tears,
But not yet settled in the fray.
He cannot cry
"Stand, Man!",
"Hope, Man!",
"Believe, Man!",
For there is a cave for these,
And he must enter there, first.
This collision,
Where daughters weep and mothers mourn,
It brings all to shambles, so let silence be.
Keep the battle inside.
Let all fret and shout
Come when within the cave, yet to come.
Man stands on neither side,
Not ill. Not mind.
The strength is not there,
Exhaled at the doctor's words,
And all that is to be lost
Is all the Man sees.
Man,
Taken by vice,
Back against the dim of light,

Once invincible,
Now none send a companion to rouse him.

____

Yes, She Purrs

She aches as she arches and stretches.
But she purrs.
Her eyes open to see who holds her and
who touches her.
She sees it is me,
and they close again.
She purrs.
Soft and old and thin, not young, still alive,
Because she purrs.
I've seen her jump, but not anymore.
I've seen her with string, but not anymore.
I've chased her, but not anymore.
I've caught her.
I've held the string.
I've searched for her.
I've heard her purr, and she still purrs.
I've seen her dependence change into love.
She purrs with me.
Here.
Now.

Suicide Note

I am weak. I'm loathe to be gentle to myself. It has
not been often I square these shoulders, stand tall,
and catch eyes with a challenge. I stare down,
knowing the landscape gives me only confusion,
only feelings of insecurity at not knowing how to
get "there". This, I have created. By leaving
willpower to chance, I am held now. An avoidable
shock I dressed myself in. I can be angry with
myself, and should be. Stunted roads are all I find,
roads I've closed in my hastily thrown tantrums
and conceit, and I've mismatched goals with my
ability. I tried beyond myself, even beyond my
worth, tried to prove the untruth, tried to convince
all that my sufficiency was real, while it lacked
greatly. The fool hearty notions I've entertained
are painful to remember. I distracted myself from
that pain, rather than learn the lessons. How can
such as I be here, when I refuse to know more
about myself and make this soul become real?
Who am I, in the face of my pretending? In misery,
I find no need of me. There is nothing to build,
rebuild, and name. Would that I could tell of hope
for the next hours, as you want, doubtless. Would
that my experience made me wiser. But there is no
experience other than backtracking, avoidance,
and cowardice, and these add up to only more of
the same. I'm on my back, daydreaming of feats,
daydreaming that I were such a man, and I am a
still waste with a million moments spent on my

back upon the floor staring at the ceiling, wishing it were full of stars, when all the while they waited for me outside. Oh, to curse my father for my position! Oh, to say he left me this way! But, his life and example, so different from mine, was a classroom I ignored, where I failed all of the tests, and knew nothing of the reality of his efforts. He wrote his words of instruction every day, without my care or attention. Curse me, not him. Blame, the only currency of the lazy, the only currency I seem to carry. I point fingers at those with sweat on their brow, and honest creations in their wake. Let this be upon your eyes and minds from my heart: I have been as dishonest and corrupt as the most evil slumlord, as the most selfish billionaire, as the cruelest of pimps, and as the genocidal general, all in my steps among you. Though I had no power, no money, no property, and no influence, I still made the heaviest of footprints, only marking what I hurt, what I damaged. I am in total regret, and lack any sense of what I must do for repentance. Let my devilry be finished, as I cannot, for all my want, lay it aside. Let my eyes dim. My time may not be up, but I am ending it, here, leading my death away from another mistake.

Competitive Need

Should I jump further?
Or, just, should I jump further than him?
Is it I that seeks to improve?
Or is it him I seek to best by being better?
Does the mind expand upon my victory
If it comes by his defeat?
Or, does my victory lie in my improvements within
my mind's victorious expansion?
While he sits in 2nd, am I better in his vanquish?
Or, am I better in my goal to be even better next
time?
Shall life stand in place, watching him succumb in
competition?
Or, shall life continue on, allowing both to prepare
for competition?

In me awakens drives, either based for myself, or
based on him.
One brings assignment of his value.
The other, elucidating my existing value.
My celebration is not at his expense,
Lest it holds me fast, not seeking the place
I want to be,
Only remaining where I am.

One Day

One day
will be the last when you wander and look,
And watch 'round the yard.
One day
your pawprint from the day before
will not be met by a new foot pad.
One day
the flowered bush you sniffed a thousand times 'fore
Will feel lonely without your nose.
One day
the wind which carried the scent that grabbed your attention
Will race along unnoticed, 'out the worth.
One day
the glance you cast at me to see if I'm with you
Will simply be a trick of my mind.
One day
I'll utter a call, the first part of your name,
Then stop short, not seeing you stand there.
One day,
But 'tis not today.
Will we have to say "Goodbye"?
Will it be forever?
Not today.
Maybe tomorrow.
Come when I need, then, like today.
May memory last and be as real,
One day.

Us, and Separation

Forgiveness, my goal,
is the bastion of my regret.
I wring my hands and stare
At the spinning fan on the ceiling.
Hear the beat of my heart drone over and above
The din.
Taste the salt-stressed sweat on my lip.
This is not a pain for a man,
It is more.
But I sinned so much, too.
I wring my hands, press my eyes closed.
I dare a prayer to remake that moment,
Turn right this time,
And a road not taken, taken.
Yet, here I am.
I wring my hands, hear your sobs,
My confession.
I am left to consider:
Did I recount because of regret?
Because of forgiveness?
Are you so dear?
Or is it what you give?
I will stay in this way, I will remain,
Wringing my hands,
To your answer, given or not.
Then, are you so dear?
Or do I need what you give?
Yes, there is regret in my mind
and there, among my feebleness, obviously.

You cry, you wail.
Am I dear? Or, do you need what I give?
I need the time to end,
But I know.
You need the time to know.

Stand Still

I weary of endings,
Of dust reclaiming dust.
Eyes closing.
Last breaths.
The stillness that stays.
It is not calm, nor kind.
I seem to wait for it to be broken,
Before it was,
In yesterdays,
When happiness and playfulness
Would rise with the sun.
They would settle my mind,
Give me comfort;
Comfort where I was needed.
Now, I sit, and I rise.
I look, and I wonder.
The old men were wrong;
Shared adventures in life
Do not make this
A moment of happy remembrance.
I ache at every flash,
Every recalled frame.
Then, yet,
Perhaps,
I am not old.
To be an old man,
To know of that mourn and suffering,
With gladness still,
May be the mark of

Satisfaction.
I hunger on for more adventure
And I lack the companions
To its whole.
But knowing what is left behind,
Knowing this,
I tell myself to wait.
The death, and the deaths,
That weigh on me,
They drag as a chain,
Stalling, then slowing,
My effort of progress.
For how can I step forward,
Over and over,
Without these that were my life,
My friends, true and sweet?
Wearied, now.
Carrying loss, unwilling.
I know my path extends,
Thinner now, but it goes on.
When exhaustion has fled
From nights of worry,
Of tears,
Of feeding empty hope,
The cinder that suffocated,
That was there in the heart,
That was raised to flames
By those who are gone,
May, yet, rise,
May, yet, urge.
So, leave me be

As I stare at the dust and the still.
Hold back your supportive hand
That intends to take me from here,
My place where I am tired
And I tarry,
Where I cannot let them flee.
Torture though it is,
I'll be an old man one day,
Then all this,
These repeated stabs of
Hard choices and cold actions,
The void where I now seek to feel,
Will mean something more.
Still, I am not old.
Still, I am not completed.

Tempted

I wish,
Deep in me where my soul won't be found,
To be beyond this moment.
To step aside.
To be as the stone in the current.
Not buffered, not tossed.
Let my own creation avoid my gaze.
I hold still,
As I should have always been.
This bright scene raises my tolerance of fear,
Makes it difficult to show it.
Can I be a child?
Can I scream, and cry, and hide?
Will this instant then forgive and desist?
There's this answer of "No" that
I give to myself.
I know "Yes" won't erase reality.
As breath, I share too much.
As sound, I was not silent.
Damn my gender.
Gone to Hell are my plans
Because these dark, male natures dig in their
hooks.
Let me try to smile through this,
Not to laugh, not to flirt.
Be hidden, Lust!
Be in my pocket,
And not on my sleeve!
We all reach out,

But it is my torture, my fall,
That I have this option to hold.
Damn my gender.
Gone to Hell is my past,
About to be traded.
Given for this moment.

Under the Boughs

I recline and consider where you are,
And where I wish you to be.
It is the moments of intertwined fingers,
Light kisses on your cheek,
Head rested upon my neck,
And my arms wrapped around your waist
Which grip my needs,
Urge this man to seek you.
You do not dance for me,
Nor cook, nor clean.
That is your way.
Though, it is you that stills my trembling,
Guides me to tomorrow.
It is you who knows me,
And my next word.
It is enough of this confidence to reside
In your love,
Given that I hear your voice each morning,
That I feel your skin against mine,
That you look me in the eyes and smile.
These decades of us,
With promises sustained and renewed,
They are my crux.
Were I to wish,
Were I to write a prayer and burn it
To make it live,
I would beg only that the affinity you show me
Can always be mine, from day to day,
Never to die,

Never to dim,
Never to deplete.
In all my words and doings,
Let my love raise you to happiness.
Be sure that age and hours
Will never be without this passion.
I would follow your pathway,
Hurdles be damned.
Endeavor to be there for and with you
As our footpaths are one in the same.
Your tears and miseries,
Every broken, peaceful moment,
I cannot erase or shield from you.
But
I will be that strength you need,
A help to repair your feelings,
A word or two,
Some boldness you need,
To believe that
Though your soul conveys this alone,
You have my presence,
And my aid,
And my faith,
Until there is a dawn that finally
Magically,
Bares your gladness.

Not On My Shoulders

Here, after,
Let me avoid your punishment.
Let me make empty amends.
Let me apologize with no true sorrow,
And tear up, trembling lip and all.
Wish I hadn't done it,
The deed.
Though, I still can't see the damage.
But, I'll bow,
Holding my head with my hands.
I'm here because you found me,
You waved and pointed your finger,
And set my excuses aside,
Found me guilty,
Without my feelings of guilt,
Until now, verdict around my neck.
So regretful you saw me,
Consequently remorseful.

Reputation

I want to hear them say
There was caring in my eyes.
That I did not watch
The troubles of others
Like I watch the landscape pass
From my speeding car.
That I both held my hand out
To steady, save,
Feed, give, entertain,
Enjoin, soothe, console.
And,
To raise my voice
— To scream —
For the rest to see
The need, pain,
Hunger, stumbles, traps,
Infirmities, callousness,
Neglect, misuse, tyranny.

I want to hear them say
That I gave sense in my daily breath,
And direction,
To this existence without instruction.
That these words have
Bridged between you and I,
And I yearned, gave you more,
That you took them in,
Made them increase beyond me.
That waves of dark musing

Did not conquer my desire
For tomorrow,
And I discovered,
Held on to,
Real bliss.

I want to hear them say
That I loved her more
Than my sight, my breath, my control.
That all these she stole when
She looked at me and grinned,
Each precious day
I was with her.
That we loved them all,
Every paw,
And made them family
To fight for, hold, tickle,
Share with,
To calm.
And, that when forever takes us,
You say that
We are where they are,
An infinite pack, roaming.

I want to hear them say
There was worth in my birth
And loss in my death.
May there be one, solitary person,
In each generation,
Passing on,
One who says my name,

For what I have given,
Beyond the words, the pages.

____

Juliet

Crying "Wherefore art thou, Romeo?"
Was tragedy in words from her,
From one taught to look outward for value.
Not within.
Feeling instinctive need,
As her own worth without him escapes her.
Time does not slip through her fingers like sand.
One must be on the beach of the ocean, the lake,
the river,
To reach for the sand,
And she was told to stay long away from these.
Her hands grip that which they give her,
And not what she must have from her dreams,
But what they must have from her.
And her worth escapes her.
With the words of her mother and father, their
trying and weighing,
She has no merit from within,
Withheld from mindfulness, at expense.
She cannot know herself for all the defining chatter
in the classroom.
"Virtue itself turns vice, being misapplied",
They told her,
And through her life, their virtue,
And in her death, their vice.
Can she be drawn towards her own significance?
By her own need?
Or, by their demand?
Or by Romeo's insistence that she be his,

And not her own? Let her be.
It was not the lesson she needed.
But it was that learnt.
"My only love sprang from my only hate."
It was the limit set before her.
It was the limit set again.
Her path to the knife, without him, would not have
been.
An option erased of others, taken by others,
And none presented for her choice.
Her own worth escaped her.

Them

How terrible are the lies we tell women.
How awful are these lies women believe.
The questions they ask about being, belonging.
Then, answers are provided,
Not given life from their hearts and minds...
Not springing from passions and hopes.
They wait for happiness from a platter,
A serving given to them,
Like hay to a mare, chewing on her bit,
Never free to be, or believe.
We hold some truth in
"Protect them from the world,
And from ruining this world."
Let that thought flee from women,
For they are the world;
They are the color in our homes,
The giggles in our ears,
The scent of warmth and flower from our candle,
The workers we need beside us,
Not beneath us.
There would be no softness in this life,
And no known comfort or ease,
Save it is seen and dreamt in their eyes, first.
They dream what we cannot,
While we tell them they cannot dream
Of any goal we hold at bay.
We would make "lonely" and "safety"
Part and parcel.
Place them secure and kept.

And we step along in this world,
Content to bring stories of this beautiful Earth
Back to them,
But do not dare to release them into that beauty.
Breakable does not imply fragility,
As steel will shatter and splinter in time.
It is not our duty to remove their bonds,
Rescue them,
And make easy their way.
Simply, do not place chains upon them.
Do not tell them where they fit,
What they shall be,
Or that their words are limited.
As man masters skill,
So shall she.
As leaders guide and assist,
So shall she.
Were we to but accept that we both,
Man and Woman,
Rose together from water to land,
Stood up,
And became man and woman,
Then, you see,
Their reach extended, as well;
Their eyes discovered, as well;
Their hunger felt, as well;
And, they survived as much, as well.
My wife, mother, my sisters, my neighbor,
Who I am not above, nor beneath,
Let me be beside you
As you show me how

You can be, and believe.

Inmate

The first time,
All over again,
the ride and walk,
… that walk,
I praise the gloom and clouds,
Feel the drops
That their God's angels pour down
Upon my face,
While looking up into the gray haze,
Toward that mist of seasons
I won't see turn again.
I march, followed and guided,
Walk with strange shoes
A bit too tight,
But they'll do for
The ride and walk.
I stare that long-way off,
Sharing the mood,
One split between self-anger
And loathing of my gatherers.
Loath, I do,
That there is a last tree to walk under,
There is a last puddle to splash with
My sole.
There is the sting of last seeing your grave
A final time,
Not knowing it was my last,
But it means everything to me now,
And I wish had placed flowers

And a kiss above you.
Now, the distance is eaten up with progress
Of my travel to the inside.
I count involuntarily
The steps I am taking with my feet,
And memorize the last mountain in my view
And the last blade of grass
Against the wall of my prison,
Cut short,
lucky in its closeness to its kind.
I'm mournful, Father.
I am sorry that your supportive embrace
Will not take me into your arms again,
Blocked with glass and stone,
Held at bay
Because I am bad.
Crime to punishment,
Punishment to loss.
The loss was always taught,
But now it is real.
Knowing that my scant view of sunlight
Will be, all, reflective,
And I won't take in the rise and set
Again while I breathe.
Angels, only you can be with me as I stand,
As I sit and lay.
Come frequent and stay
With no words,
As my mother's voice is turned to text,
And you stay, Love, in your grave.
Angels, hold the evil man in your thoughts.

Yes, allow my penance and rebuke hold me
Away from the view of your Heaven,
All the stars.
But though I deserve this,
Whisper into my hearing those details now gone.
Let me remember the wet rain.
Let me hold in the smell of her cooking.
And, let a grain of keepsake
Take me back to simple creeks and rivers
Long torrid before me,
Long flowing as I am here, and after.
By this, all,
Drown out and away the clang and bang of the
door,
The last separating me from all now memories.
As I sit and wait time, wait for my end.
Angels, prepare my next home,
For this place where I now rest brings none.
Silver and weak, I will become here.
But give me reasons to smile when I am released
To you,
Angels.

A Short While

It is ours for the taking,
But now it is gone.
We stand in it,
Watching beauty gather
And build,
But, in an instant,
What should have been done
Cannot be.
Hold to nothing,
And that is what is left for you.
There is instinct in this moment,
Full of present time,
Waiting to be followed
As a cat to a mouse,
But wait,
And, in that time,
Our eyes lose its shadow
And we are left nowhere,
Without a prize of our own.
Hold to nothing,
And that is what is left for you.
As she whispers
Her last lovings spells upon you,
And looks, weary,
Every word that could have been
Fills your mind, full,
And, though now full,
There is no time to say them all.
So, stammer now,

Speak now,
Say what can be shared now,
While her end slides over her,
And give her the moment of joy
You held back before.
Shame is the gift of waiting,
Built by knowing what was possible then,
And not at all now.
Feel shame,
But to carry it into now,
Will give it offspring that
Tug on your apron,
Making you miss what you should do
Now.
Let this time and the next be peace.
Let out your urge and act in strength.
Act in kindness and boldness,
But act now, for
Hold to nothing,
And that is what is left for you.

You're a Dog

Despite my tears, your animal eyes speak to me,
There, in your resolution, as I feel you say,
"Do not let this pain hold you back.
Do not shrink to avoid more hurt.
Do not lose this moment to give life, smiles, and
hope,
As you have given me.
Let two that live in loneliness be together,
Both happy in that bond,
Be it short, or long.
Share what I had from you,
Or lose it in waste."

The End of a Romantic Walk

I hold the pen loosely as I stare in the direction of
these papers,
I shuffle my feet, thinking of the level of warmth I
feel,
Avoiding what insists.
Get up, change the thermostat with unneeded
attention.
There's the picture of us in the corner which calls
my eyes.
No desire can overcome my pain at that urge.
No pain can quash my desire to see your happy
eyes,
Your smiling lips, your hand holding mine.
Yesterday's images overlay the moment of late,
Where you weren't happy or grinning, but
screaming, heated, reaching for solace, not
accepting my comfort.
I take my chair and sit again, realizing the
disturbance of this house's silence.
I can see the emptiness.
Not as those hours you labored your time away,
because your return was granted.
The pressure of your void stings my eyes and ears,
leaving so much to think about.
I welcome a bit of hurt of a memory here and
there,
But that bit overwhelms so quickly.
I need that sense of your blisses.

They don't exist, so far away, and I need them.
Need.
What are your words these days?
About me.
About your future.
About your losses.
What I left for you.
What is left of me?
You left. Pushed? Pulled?
In this, my answers aren't yours, and I know.
And I wish they could be.
To find your logic would thrill me, while my search
destroys me.
We had shared the emotional side.
It's not allowed now, but you can't take it away.
I can't survive on that past,
But I can feel that spark of memory with content.
Content broken by the words spoken in
jurisprudence,
Leaving no time to breathe, to plan, coordinate, or
solve.
No chance to reverse this wounding of my mind.
I won't talk of fault.
I don't know it.
I can't understand it.
I'll silently hold the conversation where you come
home.
You tell me the minutia. I nod and reply.
And you accept my presence.
So different than yesterday.
You know it.

So, you gathered and packed, Lashed out,
Bundled and claimed.
I screamed what might work to stop it all.
I stood in your way,
I promised you this world to stay, and said,
"When you leave, my fire will burn out, and I will
weep in my dark loneliness."
I sit without you;
I have no chances to collect an emotion of calm.
You've given the consequences and made them
legal.
In my many aches and wrenching,
You are held back by hate.
How do I...?
Finish that question without the ability to impact
this in the smallest amount?
I wish I could bring you back to us.
To my chair, no longer our chair.

Womb

The Robin knows the breeze
And faces it still.
Perched on a bare branch,
Safe and quiet, in rest,
She takes in her world
And even has enjoyment in it.
No predator flies above
Or stalks below,
And no threats are near,
So she is, in rest.
With closed wings and sharp eyes
And a lulled grip in her feet,
This pause from churning the air
Is welcome, welcome,
In near perfection.
Today is the day
That the Earth has created for her
Where she is content to be
Part of the beautiful landscape,
Rather that flitting about
In frantic worry
Of what else the Earth has made.
She must feel love,
Yes, it is love,
At this frozen moment of peace
Where she can embrace
Her own self
And say,
"I am a robin."

On Our Chance Meeting

The whiles of wildness,
Calling me into the fray,
Called to dance in the ferocious,
Beckoned to throw my soul in that disarray
That means everything
To me.
But you,
You felt comfortable where you were.
Our joined zest beyond the norm,
Couldn't entice you out of the brush,
Pretty hazel eyes,
With their hooks sunk in me,
Prefer the easy path,
The friends you came with,
The knowledge of safety.
Were I a younger man,
You would be my target,
You would be the one that fills my need,
Causes my spirit to believe
That my being and essence deserves more.
But you stay close to your home fire,
Away from where we can meet,
Away from that place we can hold hands,
Sticking in honey with your kin.
So, I alone flit and fly between the conversations
You pretend to be in,
As if wholeheartedly,
As if passionately.
I see you like my attention,

These ardors and compliments,
But I'm not here to stay
In my dreams.
You play light in your world,
And I keep mine at bay.
He, that is first,
It is he that gains first.
And this is life, in coincidence.
You play among options.
I strive to stand out.
You, that beautiful goal.
Me, that wanton addiction
That you avoid
To remain pure.
At least,
Pure.
You.
Life is an acrid snare
left from wars, years ago,
and yet here I stand,
ready to put my foot into your trap,
because you call me,
because you push me,
because you, such treachery,
Are interested in what you catch.
I'll step outside,
If you don't mind.
I'll find others,
Where my company they'll keep.
Yes, I mourn you,
With visions of you kissing him,

And not me.
But, dear hazel-eyed beauty,
My heart is worth the anchor you drop
And more.
The net you cast to simply see,
Explore and be thrilled, is
Meant to see what can be caught in your name.
Your perfect skin,
That inviting smile,
Mean nothing,
Where they're not given
To me.
Take them, instead.
Save them for your real intentions.
Let me wander strange patterns
While I forget you.
While I say, to that shadow you planted,
Fleeting,
I don't know what you need,
But, it's not me,
Or those like me.
Do not demand I fill the time
Between your promised,
And your leisure.
I'm not settled to you only,
So only you, truly,
Are not enough for me.
Let slip promise from your knuckles.
Be shocked at the emptiness waiting for you.
I'll not linger.
I'll march on beyond you.

Yours are the rhymes of little girls.
You feign and twirl giving me nothing to trust.
So, I'll go alone,
But I'm free, to my life and lineage,
And you are beholden to your dreams,
Those of being a princess and queen,
Leaving nothing for reality,
Leaving nothing for men.
Leaving nowhere for you to turn.
Ten paces past, I forget you.
Into the fog, you lose my love.
Play with his heart, at your will,
But mine, honest and mature,
Treated as if yours,
Is fitted for treks and vistas,
Where your childish being has no bearing,
No willpower.
So, don't assume you're my Queen.
Don't believe my smile to be devotion.
Yes, my heart is broken, because I craved your
image.
But that vision is empty,
And your worth, well, less than before.
There will be a tomorrow.
There will be an eve where you see me,
And remember, I made you feel
Amazing.
But, that memory,
That glance at yesterday,
Is all you can attain.
I am beyond you.

I am beyond you.

____

Left To My Own Devices

I can't.
I don't know how to be more,
Because
I can't possibly be less.
You may ask me,
And, believe, I'll give,
But I would borrow and beg,
Just for your illusion of me.
March on, young hope,
March away,
Until you pass from my view.
Let me know my place,
Here, among self-made muck.
If only I could give effort,
Effort to become,
Effort to change,
But I can't shake this exhaustion
That sin has brought upon me.
To be inadequate,
While so sincere,
Casts my goal to improve
Into insincere shadows and corners.
There's no one to talk to,
No empathy,
For I cannot even expect
These from my reflection.
I can't.
I don't know how to shine.
While dreaming of finery,

I donned burlap and ash,
And never once
Acknowledge that dissonance.
You are kind, as ever.
Never have you turned away
When face to face with my truth.
What is more,
How could I imagine,
At all,
That you'd detect my truth,
Let alone, accept it.
I am mad,
Twisting,
Low and defeated,
With no enemy,
No skirmish,
No war,
But only the cruelty to self.
See my plans?
See whose pretense presents?
I make a better character
Than person.
I could lie,
I would lie,
With words of "One day...",
And, though contrived and naive,
I do.
Yet, I know well this:
My perfect self
Exists inside my thoughtful mind.
It is not gestating, like in others,

Waiting for birth.
I caged it, long ago,
By my fury of wayward choices
And the exchange of good for bad.
I can't.
I don't know any more.
If you come upon a broken person
Elsewhere,
Turn your tenderness to them.
I am bronzed,
And shall never change.

Cheap Erotica

"Consume me"
Is all I can ask.
Take me in
And deliver intimacy.
Hold it above my mouth,
So that I can drink.
Dare to connect
On levels beyond
The sole.
I may sing to create rhythm,
Bring your mind to my scope,
Bring that tremble to lips,
Thighs,
Skin,
Mouth,
As you trust bit by bit
My hunger for your flesh.
That sweat,
It builds,
Focused on our pressed measures,
Hands holding your hair,
Teeth on your neck,
Feeling our heat reflect.
Changing positions brings
The agony of short breakage,
Then you engulf me again.
Finish, never.
I am evolved for your
Sounds of pleasure.

I am evolved and yearning.
Every night is the next chapter,
Written in new font
With dropped inhibitions,
And begging, "Please".
The look in my eyes,
More than love, beyond,
To where I must let you know
The movements you give
Against me
Are gifts to my soul,
By your need and passion for me.
Let me return it
While you moan to the shallow,
Then the deep.
They said it best,
But, still true,
So close to each other,
Chest to chest,
Hearts beating
Inches from one another,
Wondering why I just said that.
But, dear, come nearer.
Cum nearer.
Grip and cling on my muscles.
Caressing your curves,
Soft, all sensations,
Skin of pores,
Where my fingers drag,
Moist,
Catching slightly with salty texture.

Give you a man,
You, a welcome donor
To my self-belief,
My self-assurance,
Spurring on
My body's ache
For you.
In this second among the minutes,
I wish,
Stretching to infinite fulfillment,
That there be omnipotent perpetuity,
And on.
You whisper those words
As I lift you,
Carry you
In my arms,
Against walls and windows,
On me, in you.
Tongues, do cavort
And stop my speech,
And speak, only
Your sentiment for me.
Never to miss this,
What a promise it is,
And gaze along our sunrise,
To our sunset,
Together.
A peak,
Our crest,
As you twitch and throw,
As I scream and arch,

This, our objective;
Holding on
To live forever
In this trailing stillness
Of heavy exhales,
And ropes of me to you.
Not to cry, not to mourn
The end.
That has been our aspiration.
Never leave.
Stay on and in.
Indulge in your quaking legs
And my throbs.
Romantic words
Are on my tongue,
Yet, all would denigrate
— just below —
What
We attained
In this room.
I will not be quieted,
But I will say nothing
With those words.
Left to be the one with you.
Left to be the one.

Trēow

My Tree is not perfect
But it stays perfectly still for me
On this calm day in sun, under blue.
As small branch may quiver
When set upon by starlings,
As I sit below
And muse upon railway crossings,
funerals, new suits, pharmacies,
Treatments, and nothing more.
Bark, crisp bark,
Crackling as I slightly writhe in angst,
In my worry, hidden, hidden,
From my tree,
Falls like shed hope,
Mine and of countless men in kinship.
I can press and lean against you, Tree.
I can find shadow there
Where the solar light gives none,
All from you, my Tree.
Think on of growth and countless time.
Be my opposite now.
Be what I yearn to be.
It strikes my heart, sharp and joyous, Tree,
That when I am dust spread on a mount,
When I am erased from footnotes
In my family, in my heritage,
You will rise, and rise, and be.
While I get no hope here,
But let hope sink upon your roots,

Those, your grip upon your eternity, and
I know that you will overcome me.
Think on me, Tree,
Think on my time here,
A blink to your years,
And let my tears be in memories,
Recalled when others sit where I've been,
With their own musings of want
And they think on who came before,
For it is me.
For all, I am not lost here, below.
For all, problems are held here, below.
They weigh, they weigh, they stay,
But, here, they do not swell
As they stand before my gaze as they are now,
When I sat on this dirt plot,
Seeking nothing but you, my Tree.
If you had speech, if you had comfort to give,
I cannot hear it, and I cannot imagine it,
But speak it still, so I can wonder,
And feel soft the strength in your support.
Let me stay,
Let me shudder at the thought of standing up,
And let me stay,
And please my moments without changes
In all you give by being.
Let me become resigned here.
Death, take me within this shaded home
Where a soul is ready to be gone,
And, I, saddened, seek no more of my breath.
Let it be here, were the torture stands away,

And I define it, but can't solve it,
And let it be now.
After it all, let it be now,
Aside my Tree.

———————————————————————————

I'm Sensing a Theme

We are done.
We are done,
And we are set in place.
Final bricks bring final farewells.
The doors are shut,
And we have no paths home.
Call to me.
Let me lift my eyes to your horizon,
Where you name the dawn your own.
There, I cannot roam, else memory,
There, you beckon me,
But, I, invited, bear none to your feast.
The clay, it sets too quickly.
False features cast as my true self.
Oh, I am shallow as a man.
Oh, this life's pretense I set in foundation.
Owed, I was, to the true love.
Deserved it, you did,
By payment,
And I stole your fee.
Were I less awful,
— able to accept my place in life,
And the luck and beauty I held —
Your sweet words of forever
Would be my anchors,
And your embrace,
My fuel to this heartbeat.
But, dear Princess,
I strayed like a bastard,

Desperate for home,
While denying you,
My home.
There are highways I've traversed,
Looking,
While you were mine.
Unlike the trope,
None led back to you.
So,
When realization set in,
And I valued what
I sauntered from,
Dispassionately,
I would turn back,
Having no other choice,
Back, on that long-run road,
Back to your solace,
And the safety,
Without merit.

Untitled (Grip)

Time, be latent, in me,
In that travel between
The want to die
And
The want to kill myself.
Long, do I let the emptiness
Preserve,
Never grasping for
Happy, elsewhere thoughts.
Rather,
The still gloom of that
Does echo,
Does push and pull,
And I am there,
In revelation,
That the travel is finished.
I am here,
Where my road ends.
Only another may lift, carry,
Move, and set me
Upon any that goes on.
For, else,
I fall,
Nowhere to go.

It's All in the Eyes

I've nothing to give.
Therein, I've nothing to keep.
Strip and see that this is beyond my offering.
Strip, and be as poor as me.
All my heroes are not dead.
They have stopped being heroes.
Senza and sentient,
A last hurrah for primacy,
As my thumbs prompt a grip,
Hold a tool that,
Even momentarily,
Serves,
But then, I lay it aside,
To regroup in loneliness, without.
I sleep in a cave with my brothers,
Ready, now, to forget the disappointment.
I am ready to replace those I held in honor,
For I can't be part of that replacement.
No, I fell,
And haven't a stature.
I lean on street signs and locked doors,
Begging to be man again.
Begging with tears to something
I see in heavens and stars,
Asking to be more than the upright ape,
For, sincerely, I may be, yet, lower.
Let my fleeting time weigh heavily.
Let my soul dwell on nothing else.
I need ascension,

Without a loss to being.
I hold dear the promise of tomorrow,
And with no way the achieve it,
I only enjoy that the promise is there.
All this life and its actors, strive to more.
But the strife can be of isolation
With inward smiles and adulation,
Or, striving upon the broken backs of souls,
The weakest of gains and earns,
But, still the easiest, given the order.
I've nothing to give,
Therein, I've nothing to keep.
It is a short season to live here in this slum,
Let alone become more.

Untitled (Winded Cast-Offs)

The wind is here
And it speaks.
I have no way to reply,
But I know what it says.
"Nothing stays as set.
Nothing you've lain remains.
One day, its last crumb will spiral away.
One day, the known will not be where you left it."
So, take it at its word.
At best, what would it matter?
Foundation of yesterday,
A practice abandoned for new?
As that last plank loosens,
Loses its grip on the nail,
And flies, flutters,
Into a new dimension,
Where it means nothing,
It is beyond its appearance.

____

Noticing

Well-received is well. Ignored is without. As such, my scribbling may end, for lack of destination. Like boat without port, why have the boat? As I work to the end of each — tired of chasing the metaphor and synonym, holding current of my flow's dazzle — I think to make an end if it. Why lay bare the scars of these struggles? Why seek an audience when the cost of production bows over the repay? No, I'm not captured by vanity and pride; I seek notice. Simple notice. Perhaps the notice is not the drive, but the hope of notice, that maybe this line of emotional logic would cause the unthought to spark a heart, make deep a consideration, cause change in a life. And, then, you may hope for more of my words. But, here comes the normal, expected hum and label of "quaint", scarce a second given for a minute of my work. Scarce is the attention emotion requires, split with views of pointless jest and songs of whorish deeds, and every third word I spilt tears over is taken in too slightly. So, I toss, throw, and repent of my pen and keys, over and over, wondering alone... and still alone. But, still, I scribble. My mind demands expression, as it beats my heart a bit louder when a creative crumb leads a trail. So, in this light, maybe, the shadow may fall upon you, and set bright my true, true need. My life is my own. Into life, we are placed undeserving of reason and not conscious of the need for life.

Yet, when our eyes open each morning, we anticipate the day. Not a soul among us, not the most miserable and psychopath, hopes a bad day will come. Each moment we wake, we want to give rise to the dreams that just ended, and we want some goodness to drive purpose into every tomorrow, to make this unrequested life be a restful pleasure. My meaning is this: I write to be, or, more, to know what I can be, and what I am, more hopeful then of what I can be, sure it can be possible. Knowing yourself. Knowing you are not a simple molding of muscle and blood, working like clockwork every hour of every day until our sudden end. That is so important to my well-being. Knowing that some words I join may open these own eyes and I may say, at each day's end, "I am of worth, regardless of others thinking so." Is praise so dependent on others that my own has no value? No. It cannot be. If it were, I have no right to ask notice of others. I know depression, well enough to see when its odorous vapors rise from within me. Depression, though, is never built from the truth of others' considerations; it is founded upon the emptiness of my own self-consideration. There are days when, when I wake and see the coming day, I curse what those sunny hours would be like. So void was my value to myself, that I believed nothing of that value could be had or created by me. But, you see, I write now to change and walk away from my hateful and dreaded despite of self. I can say, as I reread my poems and stories, "This came from me. This, all, came from me." In this, there is the notice. In this, my boat has port. So, you, with a perusal of this paragraph, take it for what you will, be it as whimsy or medicated rambling. I will always pick up my pen and keys, and repent having repented them. Even if what I write sits forever in an unopened file on this device, it still came from one once worthless, out of the heart of a person who once gave up, and it is these writings that created the stairs and rungs I had to scale to be valuable to myself. So, not today. I will not make an end of it. So, even if published, found of some profitable worth to man or woman, and then to fail to gain a following — the notice I do crave, — I will muse, lament, inspire, play, condemn, and encourage on with words, even if they are also ignored. For it is this moment, when I am proud that I conjured them, that matters. I do hope they please you. But my pleasure is the start of your pleasure. Without that, you would not have my words to read. And I, doubtless would not be, had I not taken in notice of myself.

Ashen Words

Burn,
Where words put to paper
Hold other purpose,
Let them burn.
Survive on that flame
Set by Dante's Inferno
And Anne Franke's Diary,
Warmed to that moment
Where you must run down your prey.
Life is not meant to dally
Among flowers and crowns,
When breath is all you seek.
Let titles and speeches
Fall to the wayside
While seeking to nourish
The very essence of life.
Though life is colored and dressed
Well by those kindnesses
And talents,
Were you to cease, and collapse,
How would Lincoln's words of freedom
Serve you?
In that moment where you would trade
All you have for a bowl of rice
And water,
Let burn all paper and binders,
For they can be written again,
But your rhythmic pulse,
Despite every ounce of effort,

Cannot be renewed.
You cannot hold books to your chest
In a fire.
You must drop all
And run.
Run with empty arms until
Nothing pursues you,
Until nothing can chase to reach
Your still body.
Then, find your paragraphs,
Those that give meaning,
Set roses along the road,
Make birds speak above,
Define you as you breathe.

Where You Need to Be

Stay home, cries the water.
Stay and rest away from some
Audience, where you perform
Like a stage prop to their
Novella, short and out of the spotlight.
Set down the love of whiskey,
Of shimmering dresses
And lustful glances,
And stay home.
Faithful no more
Means no more faith.
No more will to be trusted
In a heart that is yours.
Sit still in your easy chair,
And be entertained in your mind,
Not the gawkers and the pushers,
Those who want you to be
Something you'll never be,
Some vision they dreamt
When sleeping it off.
Let sluts play with their hair,
Stare up and down,
And make another man
Live up to their fevered hopes,
For their path takes you only so far.
Stay home, and kiss the forehead
Of your wife, one and only,
True comfort remaining
In you being you.

Let fly your insecure identity.
Let fly your unsatisfied fantasy
And all you haven't had in your life,
Traded only, and fully,
For what you mean to her.
There is a tomorrow,
Where you will see and lament
Your wandering and your weaknesses,
All brought on by
What you read in
Those articles meant for lesser men,
And all who don't understand
Who they are.
Be man, says your heart.
Be man,
For all that matters
Holds place next to you in bed,
And you can still live on
Without all that glitz and stupidity,
With a complete promise kept
To her,
And yourself.
I cannot say more than this:
Stay home.

Love, I Need Thee Not

Slave, in your desire and drive,
Let the explosion of pleasure be.
Let goodness be a footnote
And honor not even a pause.
To attain yearning and satiate,
To let eyes set the path
Rather than maps and thoughts,
To be consumed into passion
With no inkling to flee,
Such is our definition of the soul
Evolved to your present being.
All worry stands aside and bows
As you kiss deeply
With body alight in the need
Of this, of this hunger created as
Your eyes fell upon their whole presentation.
Life's purpose is found in this,
Through the holding of their chest to your heart
And knowing that such will never be
In your future days of commitment,
Only overwhelming now, in brief,
With a voice of stone tomorrow
That will remind you
In every moment of recall and gasp,
"I lived fully for one night,
Safe in being savage with my needs."
You may love again, and strongly,
Men, and woman,
Who provide what keeps you living,

But none do capture you as that night
That brought you to life.
Need love, forever,
But do not prize it above all
The heart provides.

Unused Coffins

Our prints in the dirt are gone
And we are dust to the roots of
The pine trees that stand above.
Orion, you have a new name now,
Called by the new Being
Who came after.
Mona, our last smile,
And, Guernica, the great story,
Hold your flakes as long as you can.
Salves of comfort
— Of comfort —
We needed when the child wailed
At birth, or
When the marriage fell to pieces,
Now lost in meaning, no longer
Salves.
Ache, dust, and be in such comfort,
Knowing that we all lay together in Earth
With no one mourning our departure,
Except the Ficus in our office
And the goldfish upon the child's dresser.
We are together, all,
Those who caused this
Having no better fate.
Lives of intent, may you have gained
Your dream, or,
May you have still gained from the intent
Without final achievement.
Lives of crime, now peaceful,

Doing no more to taint humanity
And leave now our story better
For your demise.
Hopes are empty, for we cannot hope,
And fallen tears spoke our feelings
For only seconds, only upon
Absent cheeks that will never
Hold more of our expression.
Live on, in dust, you dead Army.
Lend your decay to the nourishment of
Life remaining, where capital is
Not important and payment for
Labors cannot be.
Give yourself without choice,
But with acceptance, to the days of
Sunlight that follow on and on.
Maybe a spark of us will
Continue in the elements of dust,
Speaking atoms of poetry
And indicating
Who we were, as a devilish detail,
That can, may, be saintly
If we hold on to ourselves
After the mind flinched the last muscle
And we died, and died.
To take Orion, Mona, and Guernica
With memories to our fall,
To show ourselves in our graves,
Would be glorious.
But, a valiant speck of dust
Holds the same image as

A lazy speck of dust.
To all who be in like state,
Like a graveyard set for remembrance,
Shows none of those who visit
Which ones were valiant, which lazy,
Which loved, which bound,
Which caring, which destructive,
Which holy, this
Means we are gone, with no meaning
To follow.
But this is not to say
That we never had meaning.
Dust, my brothers and sisters,
My parents, my pets, and my love,
You have had meaning,
And as you change and disappear
In this soil,
Let that meaning
That was in my mind
Be enough.

____

Untitled (Symbiosis)

Symbiosis
Is not a word for poetry.
Let poetry standing for
Craving beyond need,
Where being with
Is all that satisfies.
The cheap trade
Of giving only when
You receive;
Leave it to
The decaying leaves and roots.
Leave it to the
Tiny scavengers and
The large predators.
But, ban it from poetry.
Shun it when you encounter
The bliss of chance meetings,
Or the sweet flow
From holding hands,
Where you can live another
Day without it,
But can't go on without
The yearn.
That cheap trade
Of giving only when
You receive.
That shallow place
Where you come first,
And it covers true

Love with a thick canvas,
Giving peeks only
To your intended,
As bait
To beg give you more.
Where else can deep hurt
Come from,
If not the surface of greed
Of symbiosis?
Love, love,
Let that be your word.
Empty your mind,
And release another
From being your mealtime
Plaything.
The cheap trade
Of giving only when
You receive.
There, you will
Find no happiness,
Being filled with your
Stomach's desire
With empty heart.
Linger with the one
You love, and hold fast,
And do not give love
In measured doses
Of currency.
Only of that;
The cheap trade
Of giving only when

You receive.

____

Pickett's Fence

The rushing water.
I miss the rushing water.
The highs of spray
Settling upon my skin,
The loud lows
Of the forceful flow,
The mids of bent waves
Wrestling against
Each other;
I miss the rushing water.
Be in my eyesight, water.
Let your plays of bright
Flashes and reflections
Lull me on,
As I cannot hear your voice.
For, if you call me,
I will miss your cue,
Absent in your visual show
With overwhelming drive
To hear my name.
Along the banks.
My bowl, set for breaks in
My slow, aged jolly,
Is silent,
Though I know
No difference.
Branches,
With creak-less pointing,
Make me look up at shadow fright,

More so for the silence,
The unbelievable silence.
Walk with me
Where there should be din.
Take me where dogs might
Call my name,
Might lure me to chase
As my old limbs complain,
But not one does in my notice.
I am shut out from your song, Dad,
But look to me as you sing,
So, I may remember
That baritone and
The tiny crack of your falsetto,
And feel home, home.
No danger can rouse me,
Not impact or alarm,
Not breakage and footstep
Will I tell you about,
So, I pray you still
See my useless company
As enough.
Each day, I shudder in this void
That came upon,
And left me old
In years and
Longing,
Longing for the noises
That bothered my sleep
And brought me upright
When you entered the home.

Let me bath in water,
Scrub away itch with
Its soothing trickle,   149
See the stream drop from my hair.
But, let me hear the water.
I miss the rushing water.

There Must Be the Final Page

These phrases and ramblings
Are all I can give to you, legion.
The pages you turn were birthed
In momentum's progression
Of times.
If what I blotted brings you a new feeling,
Takes you to an unfamiliar place,
Then know I am glad.
Keep that hidden into your heart.
Keep it sacred between us.
I scribble and type not for money,
Not for auction block
Where those with millions deem my worth.
I give these words because I felt them,
And
I know you have,
Too.
Though I may be dust,
Or resting upon my couch,
Or crying over the dying body of a loved one,
All of you are like me,
And,
I — with a prayer in my mind —
Am in all of you.
Disagreements be cursed and left in the past
To waste and be forgotten.
Who I voted for never cut your value to me,
At least,
I desire that it did not

Leave that taste stuck in your throat.
They say
Adam and Eve marveled at their garden.
Let you and I do the same.
Take in all that is before you,
Because you may never tread that way
Again.
If you write, write.
If you dance and sing a new music,
Play it for your audience.
Preach love from the ground you stand on
And never require a pulpit.
Let your expressions be valuable for their sway,
And not in the price tag stuck upon them.
In experiences shared, or
Never imagined from your home,
See that the globe spins so all along
Into eternity, together.
That which you read
Came from my soul on that ride among
My stars.
Please,
Be happy
And share joy.
Share with those out of mind
— with the smallest of insects,
To the whale diving deep,
And the cows wallowing in their dung,
With the dirty cat who scrounges for food,
With the man under the bridge,
And the woman in the back

Of the limousine you drive —
Bring none a disconnection
Of that they earned at birth.
Live,
Let live.
Make the world giddy with your smile.
Make the hungry and lonely
Happy you came along.
You are special because you are here,
Alive,
And all alive are so.
If I write again
And create anew,
Let each poem
And every story stand on its own.
Let my moment of passion
Be as it is to you:
A day in this life.
I place my mark on the tree
To let you know I came this way.
Go your own way,
And mark with glad tidings.
This is not now my end,
But it is an end, for now.
Let me wave farewell,
Desiring to wave hello,
One day.

-End-

www.ingramcontent.com/pod-product-compliance
Lightning Source LLC
Chambersburg PA
CBHW061534120726
48001CB00004B/1533